MW00453598

It's a Guy Thing: Helping Guys Become Men,
Husbands, and Fathers

Workbook

It's a Guy Thing: Helping Guys Become Men, Husbands, and Fathers Workbook
Published by Guy Thing Press
P.O. Box 827
Roanoke, TX 76262

This book or parts thereof may not be reproduced in any form, stored in a retrieval system, or transmitted in any form by any means - electronic, mechanical, photocopy, recording, or otherwise - without prior written permission of the publisher, except as provided by United States of America copyright law.

Guy Thing Press books may be purchased in bulk for educational, business, fund-raising, or sales promotional use. For more information, please contact Guy Thing Press.

Please visit us at www.guythingpress.com

Copyright © 2008 by Guy Thing Press
All Rights Reserved

Printed in the United States of America

ISBN-13:   978-0-9818337-2-9
ISBN-10:   0-9818337-2-1

Contents

Part One: Let's Get Real

Part Two: Raising Kids

Part One
Let's Get Real

My Story

1. What are some of the things you must do to equip yourself to be a good husband and father?

_____

_____

_____

Looking for Dad

1. Looking for dad is one of our basic human _____.

2. Adults often come to the point in their life when they go on a search to find or discover who their _____ really is.

3. Whatever the reason to "go looking for Dad", it's a journey _____ should make.

Families Need Fathers

1. Nearly _____% of American children live in a fatherless home.

2. Those kids make up:

_____% of all youth suicides

_____% of all juveniles sentenced to state-operated institutions

_____% of all high school dropouts

_____% of all young chemical-abuse patients

_____% of all drug users

_____% of anger-driven rapists

_____% of all behavioral disorders

_____% of youths in prison

_____% of all homeless and runaway children

3. If there's no Dad in the house, or he is a non-participating member, the children are:

_____ times more likely to commit suicide

_____ times more likely to end up in a state-operated institution

_____ times more likely to drop out of high school

_____ times more likely to abuse chemical substances

_____ times more likely to commit rape

_____ times more likely to have behavioral disorders

_____ times more likely to end up in prison

_____ times more likely to run away.

"I've Got a Dad!"

1. In the story about the Cannones, who envied who and why?

_____

_____

_____

2. Kids who don't have sound parenting love to hang around people with _____ parents.

3. They want to be part of a _____ place that's full of _____ and affirmation.

Not an Optional Extra

1. We supply things that are totally different to what children get from their _____.

2. As a dad, you _____ your children's world!

Dads Can Demolish Lives

1. What kind of power does a dad have in the lives of his children?

_____

_____

_____

2. How many generations does it take to make a change in the world?

_____

Embrace it, Don't Run from it!

1. If you're a Dad, you're _____ your children, _____ after your own _____.

2. _____ his children with the good things in his _____ is the greatest work on earth a man can ever do.

> _Early in my fathering career, I thought I was just an accessory in my children's lives... my partner's helpmate in parenting._
>
> -STEVE BIDDULPH

Turn This World Around

1. If _____ men decide they're going to be fathers to their families, we can literally turn this world around.

2. We can see from the statistics that it is the _____ who frames the generation.

Fatherhood - A Gift from Dad

1. Most gang members come from homes where there is a _____ but no _____.

2. A father has to be a biological father to impact a child's life.

     True   False

3. A father takes the time to sit down and bring _____ to the _____ and _____ of a child.

4. Protection isn't the macho concept of beating up the bad guys. It might be as simple as protecting someone from the wrong _____, or steering them from destructive _____ and helping them make _____ ones.

5. What three things should a father do for his family?

_____

_____

_____

6. As practical men, we are tempted to _____ things for our kids, to bring a _____ check when our kids start shotgunning _____ dreams and visions.

7. Kids are usually only looking for a dream that will _____ them.

8. A father brings three things out of his being and offers them freely to his family: _____, _____, and _____.

If you have never been hated by your children, you have never been a parent.

-BETTE DAVIS

Your Family Owns You

1. As fathers, we are right at the _____ of the list in terms of personal rights.

2. Our family gets to _____ us. We get to _____ them.

3. How do two become one flesh?

_____

_____

_____

4. You're only a leader to the degree you're prepared to _____.

5. You can only lead by _____ your family.

Include Them in Your World

1. Kids will do what you want to do.

    True   False

2. Children want _____ time.

A Hero, Not an Icon

1. There's a time in every Dad's life when he stops being _____.

2. Icons are _____, _____, and _____.

3. Dads love being _____. That's great, because kids need _____.

4. It's not about proficiency; it's about _____. It's about your being secure at being a hero and not needing to be a _____.

Fathers, Not Coaches

1. A coach is _____ for what he does.
A father _____ what he does.

2. A coach is a professional _____.
A father is a dedicated _____.

3. A coach has an _____.
A father has a _____.

4. A coach _____ you.
A father gave _____ to you.

5. A coach will _____ you from the side if you don't cut it.
A father will never _____ you or _____ you.

6. A coach will select you _____ on performance.
A father will love you _____ of performance.

7. A coach will _____ teams.

A father _____ up the team.

8. A coach is in it for the _____.

A father is in it for the _____ _____.

9. A coach _____ from the sideline.

A father _____ in the locker room.

10. A coach is responsible until the _____ of the season.

A father is responsible for a _____.

One father is more than a hundred schoolmasters.

-ENGLISH PROVERB

Fatherhood - Not a Spectator Sport

1. The family unit was designed to be the _____ of a man's world, not an _____.

2. The best way to make sure you have time for your kids is to _____ schedule them in.

3. Children with a passive dad are better off than children with an involved single parent.

    True   False

4. Engaging is not hard work; it's just an _____.

5. Engagement is about all the _____ things — a whole series of _____ moments rather than large landmark events. It's the _____ things that make the difference.

6. When we're too busy doing the _____ to engage in the _____. We become _____ of our children's growth, not _____ in it.

7. Take a few minutes to write out a plan for how you will become actively involved in your children's lives.

_____

_____

_____

_____

_____

_____

_____

_____

_____

_____

_____

Quality Versus Quantity

1. Kids need a mixture of _____ and _____ time.

2. If you, as a father, want to put your children ahead of the vast majority of the population, all you have to do is _____ your children's mother and actively _____ your kids and _____ with them.

Being male is a matter of birth. Being a man is a matter of choice

-BEN KINSLOW

Adjusting the EQ

1. If you have a _____ EQ, you need a _____ IQ to succeed in life.

2. If you have a _____ EQ, you only need an _____ IQ to succeed.

3. IQ is the result of _____; EQ is the result of life's _____.

4. That means virtually _____ man can succeed as a father, if he's committed to emotionally _____ with his family.

5. What happens to a child when there is not constant interaction?

_____

_____

_____

Father - More Than a Friend

1. You will never have conflict with your children.

    True   False

2. Who is supposed to handle character issues with your children?

_____

3. Why should you be a father instead of being a friend?

_____

_____

_____

Responsible for Responsibility

1. If you fail to warn your children of their character issues, who is accountable for the outcome of their lives?

_____

Four Steps to Fatherhood

1. Name the four steps to fatherhood.

_____

_____

_____

_____

2. _____ _____ is the ultimate rite of passage for a man.

3. What are two possible ways a man's character can change when he has children?

_____

_____

_____

Victims No More

1. Maturity is not an issue of _____. It starts with the acceptance of _____.

Your Past Will Confine or Refine You

1. If you refuse to accept responsibility for your life, your past will put you in a _____. If you take responsibility for it, though, that same past will help you and _____ you and make you into who you are _____ to be.

2. When we accept where we have _____ _____, we truly value where we are today.

3. We're not trying to be _____ Dads, we're trying to deal with our _____.

> *Fathers, like mothers are not born. Men grow into fathering - and fathering is a very important stage in their development.*
>
> *-DAVID M. GOTTESMAN*

Saying Sorry, Asking for Forgiveness

1. Out of apology comes _____, and from _____ grows _____.

2. The idea that it's weak to ask for forgiveness is rooted in _____.

3. A culture doesn't just happen. You _____ a culture.

4. To _____ a culture, behavior has to be _____.

5. Saying sorry allows a child out of all consequences.

    True   False

Breaking the Cycle

1. It is human to repeat _____ from one generation to the next.

2. A _____ is a solemn agreement that is binding on all parties.

3. Covenant-breaking sin may rob your family line for _____ to _____ generations.

4. One man's decision to get right with God takes effect then and there and it touches a family forever. It breaks the cycle of the broken-hearted for up to _____ generation.

5. If we really see fatherhood as a commitment from day one, then we need to be prepared to develop _____ in ourselves.

6. Describe the process of collective wisdom.

_____

_____

_____

7. We should limit our source of wisdom to only one source.

True   False

Parenthood remains the greatest single preserve of the amateur.

-ALVIN TOFFLER

Flight Check

1. What three gauges should we always be checking?

_____

2. On what levels should each gauge register?

_____

3. Without checking our gauges, life can become unbalanced.

     True   False

4. In what way does a dad provide security?

_____

5. What are some ways you can be there for your kids?

_____

_____

_____

An Everyday Commitment

1. As fathers, one of the areas we must take responsibility for is _____.

2. Who should pay the price when it comes to spending time with your children?

_____

On-the-Road Rules

1. How often should you interact with your wife and kids while you are on the road?

_____

2. What are some ways you can interact with your family when you cannot be there physically?

_____

_____

_____

3. When at home we should give our children as much _____ attention as possible.

4. What is a good ratio for days at home compared to weeks on the road?

_____

5. Have open _____ with your family about travel plans.

6. Being an absent father isn't about being divorced. It's about being _____.

   My father used to say, "let them see you and not the suit. That should be secondary."

   -CARY GRANT

Sometimes, Someone Else Needs to be There

1. How long do we have our children?

_____

2. One thing our children really need is a source of _____ and _____ to help them chart a course through life.

3. As their father you should be the strongest _____. But there should be other _____ too.

4. These trusted family friends will _____ what you would have said.

Dads and Careers

1. We see prosperity as how much _____ we can put in the bank. Shouldn't it rather be the whole _____ of our lifestyle?

2. As men we've been raised and cultured to believe that _____ _____ is the most significant and important thing.

3. Family has to be rated _____ among our successes and achievements.

4. If you were to rate your success in family like you score your golf game or racquetball, how would you score?

_____

Generation Xcellence

1. If you see people as _____, then you realize that corporations are _____ to be able to _____ people.

2. A person whose _____ life is in balance functions much better as a _____ employee.

3. How can you have a family and a career?

_____

_____

_____

Permission to Break the Chains

1. What things can you do to have permission to love your family?

_____

_____

_____

_____

2. Where does this permission come from?

_____

3. Many large organizations lose sight of the value of the individual as a _____ person. They see an individual as a _____ that fulfills a _____ from 8am till 6pm.

4. Because organizations don't see the whole picture, they expect you to give your _____ for the corporate vision.

5. The _____ world view has its starting point in the relationship between _____ and Man, which then expanded into God and _____. Only after that relationship was firmly established did God give Man the instruction to have _____ over the world.

Declaring Independence

1. What are some things that may hinder you from your commitment to family?

_____

_____

_____

Downsizing for a Bigger Soul

1. Most of us grew up seeing our parents go after the _____ _____. That's what we learned, so most of us are doing the _____ _____ now. It's a _____ and we're willingly caught in it.

2. What is one way to improve the quality of your life?

_____

3. Why have many people "checked out" of the corporate system?

_____

_____

_____

What Are We Doing it For?

1. We use most of our money simply to _____ us to do the things that _____ us.

2. Restricting our money flow means we can never have fun.

    True   False

3. What are some ways to have fun on a budget?

_____

_____

_____

Fathers Can Transform Families

1. A child gets a sense of uniqueness and value from their _____ with their Dad.

1. If you allow a child to throw a tantrum at three years of age, they will still be doing it at _____.

2. Parents must get involved in this sort of _____ behavior — do what it takes to get their _____ back on track.

3. One absentee Parent is tragic enough - two absentee parents result in the _____ of children's lives.

It's Not Over Until It's Over

1. If you are prepared to be Dad, if you are prepared to _____, there will come a time when your children will come back around.

2. Godly sorrow brings _____.

3. You _____ what you _____.

Relationship First Aid

1. What are some ways to repair your relationships?

_____

_____

_____

The Power of "Remember When..."

1. Why is "remember when" so powerful?

_____

_____

_____

2. We tend to see our life as a collection of emotional _____ or _____.

Give me the child until the age of seven and I will give you the man.

-JESUIT PROVERB

Creating Character

1. List the three things that a father is.

_____

_____

_____

2. We have a tendency to nurture rather than scar them.

    True   False

3. A positive, giving world view is something we have to actively _____ for ourselves.

4. If you are raising your child in an environment of constant criticism, hostility, ridicule and shame, then you shall reap an _____ and _____ child.

Monkey See, Monkey Do

1. As humans, we can avoid making mistakes.

    True   False

2. What is one way you can teach your children positive character traits?

_____

_____

_____

The Most Important Year in a Child's Life

1. When is it best to start creating character?

_____

2. If you haven't laid a good foundation with your children by a certain age, it's too late.

    True   False

3. Which year is the most important in a child's life?

_____

What Kind of Kids Do You Want?

1. A father's thoughtfulness or thoughtlessness will be _____ in his children.

2. Discipline is about _____. It's about teaching children to live within an _____ world that is also occupied by _____ people.

3. Describe the two attitudes listed in the book, that you can teach your children.

Respectful

_____

_____

_____

Appreciative

_____

_____

_____

Day Care Night Chaos

1. What do children genuinely need when they seek attention?

_____

_____

_____

Fabulous Fathers can be Deadly Dads

1. Children, although little, are still _____.

2. Describe the differences in the ways David raised his sons Solomon and Absalom.

_____

_____

_____

No Such Thing as a Cookie-Cutter Kid

1. You have to tailor your message to the _____ of the child.

2. Every child is desperate to be _____ by their peers, so as adults we often find ourselves doing things that _____ our children. If this seems to be happening all the time, though, then your child probably has an issue with _____ and _____.

3. We have to deal with each child in the way that is uniquely _____ to them.

4. Rules without relationship lead to _____.

If a child lives with criticism, she learns to condemn.

If a child lives with hostility, she learns to fight.

If a child lives with ridicule, she learns to be shy.

If a child lives with shame, she learns to feel guilty.

If a child lives with encouragement, she learns confidence.

If a child lives with praise, she learns to appreciate.

If a child lives with approval, she learns to like herself.

If a child lives with acceptance and friendship,

She learns to find love in the world.

-DOROTHY LAW NOLTE

Part Two
Raising Kids

The Way He Should Go

1. One of the miracles of families is how two parents can produce genuinely _____ children.

> *Bring up a child in the way he should go and he will not depart from it*
>
> *Proverbs 22:6*

2. Some have misinterpreted this verse to mean _____ a child so they become a certain sort of person. In reality, however, it means to _____ the gifts that are in a child and then raise the child in the context of those gifts, to help the child discover the _____ that grows from his or her own _____.

3. The way a child should go is the same for every child.

      True   False

Six Keys To Raising Kids

1. List the six keys to raising kids.

_____

_____

_____

_____

_____

_____

2. How can you be an open communicator?

_____

_____

_____

3. When talking to our children about sex, we should also dicuss modesty.

    True   False

4. How can you tune in to your child's world?

_____

_____

_____

You have to do your own growing, no matter how tall your grandfather was.

-IRISH PROVERB

Don't Do It, Dad

1. What are the don'ts of parenting?

_____

_____

_____

2. Children don't need to know about the state of your marriage, your job or your finances — unless they can make a _____ and help _____ the situation.

3. A child doesn't know the difference between a broken _____ and a _____.

The Rites of Passage

1. Maturity is not about _____; it's about the acceptance of _____.

2. List some of the hallmarks of maturity.

_____

_____

_____

3. What are some ways you can celebrate hallmarks with your children?

_____

_____

_____

4. Every rite of passage should be a _____ one.

Fathers Are Fun

1. During the newborn to crawling stage, children will interact with their _____ most,

but it is important for you as a father to become _____ early.

2. Children in the _____ stage love it if you get down to their level to be with them, banging balls on tables and floors.

3. In what stage do you begin reading with your child?

_____

4. What are ways to get involved in developing a child's imagination?

_____

_____

_____

5. When do physical activities become important to a child?

_____

The Five "A"s of Adolescence

1. Briefly describe each of the five "A"s of adolescence.

Awareness

_____

_____

Attraction

_____

_____

Appreciation

_____

_____

Anxiety

_____

_____

Acceptance

_____

_____

My father was an amazing man. The older I got, the smarter he got.

-MARK TWAIN

Protecting Your Children...From Their Friends

1. When you protect your children by cutting off poor influences, you set them on a new _____ that bears _____ fruit.

2. As parents we have a responsibility and a right to choose our children's _____ and facilitate positive _____, until our children are old enough to make _____ and wise judgments of their own.

3. Bad _____ corrupts good _____.

4. How can you create a positive environment for your children and their friends?

_____

_____

_____

5. Your children will always share your dreams.

      True   False

6. Your kids will model what you _____ them.

Physical Affection - Kids Need It; Don't Fear It

1. Kids need constant _____ attention.

2. Why does a cuddle meet emotional needs? There's the security of being _____. When a child comes for a cuddle and is _____, they experience something wonderful: the complete opposite of _____.

3. There is nothing wrong with clean, wholesome _____.

> *The position of the father is the thankless provider for all, and the enemy of all.*
>
> *-J. AUGUST STRINDBERG*

The Majority of Men - Healthy & Wholesome

1. The _____ of men are good, healthy, balanced, whole human beings.

2. Society's focus is on the perverted _____, and the rest of us allow ourselves to be _____ in those terms.

Your Daughter Will Marry a Man Like You

1. In what areas should you daughter have a level of expectation when approaching her search for a husband?

_____

_____

_____

Discipline - Pulling the Weeds

1. Discipline is not about _____ kids. It's about pulling the _____ stuff out of a potentially _____ garden.

2. Name some weeds that need to be pulled out of a child's life.

_____

_____

_____

The Keys to Family Discipline

1. List the keys to family discipline

_____

_____

_____

_____

_____

_____

Dad: The Enforcer

1. A mother is a natural _____. A father is a natural _____.

2. When a mother has to raise a child on her own, she loses the whole natural element of _____ and _____ in her family unit.

3. How can you affirm the authority of your wife?

_____

_____

_____

4. If a father tolerates bad behavior, then he is reinforcing the idea that _____ is okay.

A man's children and his garden both reflect the amount of weeding done during the growing season.

-UNKNOWN

Thoughts on Discipline and Rewards

1. If it's done with love — and consistency — in a caring environment, _____ _____ is a very effective way to enforce important rules and values.

2. It's okay to discipline your child when you are angry.

   True   False

3. What are some alternatives to physical discipline?

_____

_____

_____

4. Why is rewarding good for your children?

_____

_____

_____

ABC, Consistently

1. _____ + _____ + _____ = Discipline

2. Verbal abuse can sometimes be worse than physical abuse.

    True   False

3. Applaud in _____, correct in _____.

Honoring the Cofounder of Your Family - Their Mother

1. Your wife is your best _____ and your best _____.

2. If you love your wife, you'll treat her _____ than you treat yourself.

3. Christ was a poor leader because he was a servant leader.

    True   False

4. Children do really want to see a loving _____ between their parents.

5. What are some ways you can honor your wife?

_____

_____

_____

Like Father Like Son

1. If you are the father of sons, your boys will grow up either knowing how to treat a _____, or not knowing. It's up to you: the way you treat the number-one woman in their life, their _____.

2. Teach your children by your _____.

3. Ladies love to talk, so _____ your wife and talk to her. When she calls you at work or on the cell phone, understand that there's something she wants to _____. Listen to those words. _____ what you're doing and _____ her.

4. Things in our marriage start out as small _____ and grow into good things or bad things.

You Can Be a Fantastic Father

1. Just because you have always reacted a certain way doesn't mean you have to continue that way.

    True   False

2. We don't have to let the past _____ our destiny! We can actively choose to let the baggage go and _____ the script for our _____.

It is easier for a father to have children than for children to have a real father.

-POPE JOHN XXIII

Resources of Interest

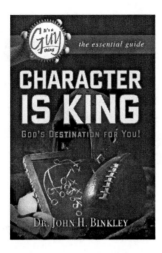

Character is King
Dr. John Binkley

It's a Guy Thing: Character is King takes you on your dream journey. There is a place called destiny that we all journey to. We all have ideas, dreams and vision for what life should be. This book lays out a plan for that journey to realizing your dreams, and to your destiny.

Let's Talk About Sex
Dr. John A. King

Let's face it. Sexuality is all around us. It's even on billboards, magazines and television commercials. Sadly, It's a topic many men and women have to deal with on their own because too many churches or pastors won't touch it. Find out what the Bible has to say about some of the toughest questions in *Let's Talk About Sex.*

Now to Next
Dr. John A. King

What does the next generation church look like? Who are the people that will be involved in the next generation church? How will it come about?

Those are some of the questions answered in Dr. King's newest release, *Now to Next: Blueprint for a Christian Revolution.*

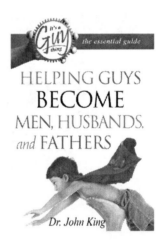

Helping Guys Become Men, Husbands, and Fathers
Dr. John A. King

It's a Guy Thing takes you on the journey of fatherhood. Dr. John King shares the skills necessary to become a good father. He shows you what can happen when a father is absent or simply not active in a child's life. Being a male is a matter of birth. Being a man is a matter of choice. This book will help you make that choice.

To see all the titles available through Guy Thing Press, visit us online at www.guythingpress.com

Resources of Interest

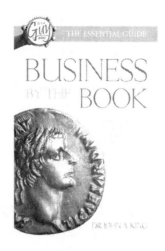

Business By The Book
Dr. John A. King

The world's greatest handbook on leadership, economic and social excellence is not found in schoolbooks, but in Scripture. The principles in this book are tried, proven and resilient over centuries. Christ bet His life on it, and so can you.

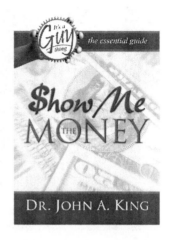

Show Me the Money
Dr. John A. King

Time Magazine asked, "Does God want you to be rich?" The answer to that question is simply "No, God wants you to be *wealthy*." In *Show Me the Money*, you will learn the fundamentals of creating and using wealth in God's kingdom.

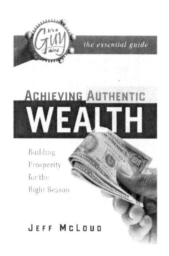

Achieving Authentic Wealth
Jeff McLoud

We need a vision that goes beyond our ability to be consumers only. A vision so big, so powerful, that we cannot even accomplish it in our own lifetime - a vision founded from the very heartbeat of God. We could see the vision fulfilled if we ask ourselves a simple question: "How can we achieve twice as much with half the money?"

Creating a Better Life
Erik A. Kudlis

In this easy to read manual, educator and administrator turned international businessman, Erik Kudlis, identifies three vital keys you must know and use, given by God Himself, that unlock the doors to the life God has always wanted you to have.

To see all the titles available through Guy Thing Press, visit us online at www.guythingpress.com

Further Resources

The Godly Man Curriculum

The Godly Man Curriculum is designed to train men from all walks of life, giving them a firm foundation of doctrine and Godly knowledge. This curriculum is available both over the internet for individual study and on DVD for seminars, Sunday schools, and men's meetings. With up to 7 hours of video teaching divided over numerous topics, the Godly Man Curriculum is an excellent tool that you can build your classes upon and grow yourself and your people.

Listen to sample teachings from the Godly Man Curriculum at www.imnonline.org.

Building Iron Men &
Life As Leaders Networks

The Building Iron Men and Life as Leaders networks are two of IMN's finest resources. Each network provides you with a new teaching every month that will challenge and encourage you to grow. The Building Iron Men network features three teachings in both CD and DVD format that are tailored for men, while the Life as Leaders network provides you with three CDs that teach leadership principles anyone can use.

Both networks are phenomenal tools that are vital assets to any church and discipleship program.

Also check out these websites for great resources and training materials.

International Men's Network
www.imnonline.org

Guy Thing Press
www.guythingpress.com

INTERNATIONAL
MEN'S NETWORK

The International Men's Network was founded by Dr. John A. King. Its purpose is to help men grow to become the leaders their families and churches need and become men of God that make a lasting impact on those around them.

IMN is a missionary organization to the men of the world. We are committed to:

- Inspire all men to rise to a high standard of biblical manhood.
- Encourage them to excel in their roles as men, leaders, husbands, and fathers.
- Challenge them to be contributors to society and set an example based upon a biblical value system that will benefit this generation and lay a solid foundation for the next generation.

The International Men's Network is dedicated to providing and hosting the best resources for men, including teachings and lessons on CD and DVD and conferences that teach men the principles that will help them become more influential and effective in their lives.

For more information about IMN and its mission, visit us online at www.imnonline.org or call 817.993.0047

christian LIFE center

cosmos | casus | christus

The Christian Life Center was founded by Dr. John King and his wife, Beccy. With a vision to preach the gospel of Jesus Christ with unashamed passion and uncompromising truth, Christian Life Center aims to raise up the next generation of leaders to move into all the world and proclaim the truth of Christ to the lost and broken.

Located in the Keller, Texas area, the church sits in the prime location to reach the community and the people therein. The church desires to give back to the community by providing outreaches to better and enrich its inhabitants. From kickboxing classes that are aimed at teaching children and adults self-defense, to a special service that commemorates and honors our country's war-time heroes, Christian Life Center strives to bring a living Jesus to a dying world by new and imaginative means that will bless and change lives.

For more information about Christian Life Center and the resources it offers,
visit the website at www.clctx.org

CPSIA information can be obtained at www.ICGtesting.com
Printed in the USA
BVOW06s1309220514

354167BV00002B/110/P

9 780981 833729